SALVATION

WHAT JESUS COMMANDS ABOUT SALVATION

By
Marshall Smith

TATE PUBLISHING, LLC

Salvation: What Jesus Commands About Salvation by Marshall Smith

Copyright © 2005 by Marshall Smith. All rights reserved.
Published in the United States of America
by Tate Publishing, LLC
127 East Trade Center Terrace
Mustang, OK 73064
(888) 361–9473

Book design copyright © 2005 by Tate Publishing, LLC. All rights reserved.
No part of this publication may be reproduced, stored in a retrieval system or transmitted in any way by any means, electronic, mechanical, photocopy, recording or otherwise without the prior permission of the author except as provided by USA copyright law.

Scripture quotations marked "NKJV" are taken from the New King James Version. Copyright © 1982 by Thomas Nelson, Inc. Used by permission. All rights reserved.
Scripture quotations marked "NIV" are taken from the *Holy Bible, New International Version* ®, Copyright © 1973, 1978, 1984 by International Bible Society. Used by permission of Zondervan Publishing House. All rights reserved.

ISBN: 1-59886-07-2-0

Acknowledgements

Those I would like to thank:

My parents, Jack and Opal Smith, for their encouragement and belief in me through victories and failures. My wife, Cindy, for her unselfish love, and commitment to me and the ministries God has called us to. Boot, our son, for giving up so much so I could attend college.

John States for introducing me to Jesus. Max and Carol Kelley, Hap and Zen Thompson and so many friends and associates for mentoring me in my Christian adventure.

By far and away I am most thankful to Jesus, God's Son, who loved me in spite of my sin. It is to Him I give all the glory and praise.

Foreword

There could be no greater interest for all humanity than to be able to answer the question, "What must I do to be saved?" Likewise there can be no greater peace than to know that by the grace of God you are walking in salvation. Since salvation is of the Lord, He is the only one who can tell us what we must do to be saved. To trust and obey is the only way to have this certainty and peace.

I have been troubled by the statements of many who claim to have such a strong faith in the work of Jesus that they don't need to obey him. This is hypocrisy at its worst. To confess with your mouth that Jesus is Lord and not surrender to His Lordship and still presume to be saved and a follower of Christ is not only unscriptural but is a deadly deception that I fear many will follow to their destruction.

Jesus exposes this kind of hypocrisy

when He says, "But why do you call Me 'Lord, Lord,' and not do the things which I say?" Luke 6:46 (NKJV) and again, "Not everyone who says to Me, 'Lord, Lord,' shall enter the kingdom of heaven, but he who does the will of My Father in heaven," Matt. 7:21. (NKJV).

The apostles are also witnesses to this truth, both pointing out the positive outcome of obedience to Christ and the negative to those who are not. He (Jesus) "became the author of eternal salvation to all who *obey* Him," Heb. 5:9 (NKJV) (emphasis added) and " . . . taking vengeance on those who do not know God, and on those who do not *obey* the gospel of our Lord Jesus Christ," 2 Thess. 1:8. (NKJV)

During this time when obedience is being sacrificed in the name of "faith only", I am thankful for Marshall's conviction to draw our attention back to the words of our Lord Jesus, showing that He does give us imperatives concerning our greatest interest—salvation.

While it is also possible to *err* and swing the pendulum to the side of "works", sacrificing faith in Christ for a trust in ourselves, I know this is not the intention or the heart of the author.

Having had the privilege to learn and grow underneath Marshall as a student in his classroom and also to minister beside him at WestWay Christian Church, I can confidently recommend Marshall Smith to you as a man who loves the Lord Jesus and desires for all to love Him, honor Him and obey Him because He is worthy and because salvation is found in no one else.

May the Lord Jesus use this offering of Marshall's to challenge, convict, and comfort, so that many, in faith, will confess and surrender to Jesus as Lord.

To God be All the Glory,

Aaron Prohs, Professor
Summit Christian College,
formerly Platte Valley Bible College

CONTENTS

Foreword............................5

Introduction........................11

Chapter One • The Short Version.........15

Chapter Two • "You Lead, Lord".........25

Chapter Three • Believe................29

Chapter Four • Repentance..............35

Chapter Five • Confess.................41

Chapter Six • Baptism..................49

Chapter Seven • Infant Baptism.........57

Chapter Eight • Sinner's Prayer........67

Chapter Nine • From Non-Christian To
   Christian In The Bible..............73

Conclusion.............................83

Introduction

Since I have been involved in evangelism, I keep hearing the same questions over and over again. "What is baptism?" "I was baptized as a baby—isn't that good enough?" "I said the sinner's prayer after listening to a T.V. evangelist. He said I was saved."

I have visited with many pastors, reverends, and priests; read many handouts and books; visited revivals and seen people shouting hell-fire and damnation on the street. There are many schools of thought on salvation. If we just listen to one school, presented by someone with passion, it all seems to make sense. As a teacher, I will have a stricter judgment for what I teach others about God and His plan for the lost. In the Bible, the book of James, chapter 3:1, we read:

"My brethren, let not many of you become teachers, knowing that we shall receive a stricter judgment." (NKJV)

The first question we each need to ask is, "What is the most important fact in the Bible?" Paul answers this in I Corinthians 15:3–4:

"For what I received I passed on to you as of first importance: that Christ died for our sins according to the Scriptures, that He was buried, that He was raised on the third day according to the Scriptures." (NIV)

Nothing will ever be more important than the facts that Jesus died for our sins, He was buried and He was raised from the dead. This is the key—the Gospel message is only complete when we come to the realization that Christ's love and God's love supersedes everything else. The reason we are to be obedient to Jesus comes from our desire to have a personal relationship with Him.

To put anything before the gospel or to do anything out of a "works motive" is wrong. It is by grace and divine love that we are to come to Jesus, knowing it is His blood that was shed so we can have the free will to choose to be obedient to what He commands.

It is time we get back to the plain truth which Jesus died for and teaches through the gospel. As you study, remember, it is Jesus who is giving the commands, the instructions, the promise of blessings and heaven as you are obedient to Him. It is my prayer that you follow Him and that He, Jesus, will receive all the glory.

Note to reader: Throughout this book the words of Jesus will appear in bold for emphasis.

Marshall Smith

Chapter One
The Short Version

ONLY ONE WAY!

John 14:6 Jesus said to him, **"I am the way, the truth, and the life. No one comes to the Father except through Me."** (NKJV)

Jesus is the *only* way to the Father—the *only* way to Heaven. Jesus being the only way to Heaven, we are to be obedient in what He commands for our salvation.

To Go Deeper, See Chapter Two

BELIEVE:

John 6:47 **"Most assuredly, I say to you, he who believes in Me has everlasting life."** (NKJV)

John 8:24 **"Therefore I said to you that you will die in your sins; for if you do not believe that I am He, you will die in your sins."** (NKJV)

Do you believe Jesus is the Son of God?
(Yes)   No

To Go Deeper, See Chapter Three

REPENT:

Have you ever sinned?
(Yes)   No

Then, you need to repent.

Luke 13:5 **"I tell you, no; but unless you repent you will all likewise perish."** (NKJV)

To Go Deeper, See Chapter Four

CONFESS:

Mathew 10:32–33 **"Therefore whoever *confesses* Me before men, him I will also *confess* before My Father who is in heaven. But whoever *denies* Me before men, him I will also *deny* before My Father who is in heaven."** (NKJV - emphasis added)

If I <u>CONFESS</u> Jesus, He will <u>CONFESS</u> me. If I <u>DENY</u> Jesus, He will <u>DENY</u> me.

To Go Deeper, See Chapter Five

BAPTISM:

Mathew 28:18–20 And Jesus came and spoke to them, saying, **"All authority has been given to Me in heaven and on earth. Go therefore and make disciples of all the nations, baptizing them in the name of the Father and of the Son and of the Holy Spirit, teaching them to observe all things that I have commanded you; and lo, I am with you always, even to the end of the age. Amen."** (NKJV)

Mark 16:16 "**He who believes and is baptized will be saved; but he who does not believe will be condemned.**" (NKJV)

Jesus tells us to be baptized.

BURIED WITH CHRIST IN BAPTISM:

Romans 6:3–4 "Or do you not know that as many of us as were baptized into Christ Jesus were baptized into His death? Therefore we were buried with Him through baptism into death, that just as Christ was raised from the dead by the glory of the Father, even so we also should walk in newness of life." (NKJV)

Colossians 2:12 " . . . buried with Him in baptism, in which you also were raised with Him through faith in the working of God, who raised Him from the dead." (NKJV)

When we bury something we completely cover it up. The words for sprinkle or pour in the Greek are never used in the Bible concerning baptism. In every instance where the word baptize appears in the Bible, you can replace it with immerse.

Have you been baptized into Christ? Baptism is how you begin a relationship with Christ. It is no more important than belief, repentance, or confession. We are commanded by Jesus to do all four.

To Go Deeper, See Chapter Six

Jesus, being the only way to the Father, misses no words in giving us directions to follow.

Believe (John 6:47)
Repent (Luke 13:5)
Confess (Mathew 10:32–33)
Be baptized (Mark 16:16)

Which of these commands is the most important? Which of these commands is the least important? They are all given by Jesus. Not one is more or less important than the other. Jesus being the only way to the Father, we are to be obedient in *all* of His instructions. Obedience is the first step of a relationship with Christ which will continue to grow and mature.

The Short Version Notes

Chapter Two
"You Lead, Lord."

The scripture which this study must stand on is John 14:6.

John 14:6 Jesus said to him, **"I am the way, the truth, and the life. No one comes to the Father except through Me." (**NKJV)

Now let's take a deeper look at John 14:6. There are four key elements in this Scripture.

"I am the way." When Jesus says this to me it is the same as saying He is the path or the door. He is the *only* One we are to follow, to trust and to guide us into Heaven.

"I am the truth." Webster's College

Dictionary defines truth *as a verified or indisputable fact.* Jesus is the Son of God, holy and pure. He is the creator and author of truth. He is the standard on which everything will be judged. Without God, Jesus, Holy Spirit, and the Bible, there is no standard for truth.

"I am the life." I believe Jesus is saying that He is real life, supernatural life, eternal life, all of which are greater than any life of any human here on earth. The life we will have in Heaven can only come from Jesus.

" . . . no one comes to the Father except through Me . . ."

What is He saying? Who can get you to the Father? Can:

Buddha? _NO_
Mohammed? _NO_
Mary? _NO_
Who is the only one who can get

you to the Father? _JESUS_

There is one and only one way to God—through His Son, Jesus. Do you believe Jesus is the way, the truth, and the life, and the only way to God and Heaven? Yes or No.

So, let us move forward as we are in agreement that Jesus is the only way to Heaven. The question we must ask now is what does Jesus say or command for us to have salvation? We must turn to His words, or what I like to refer to as "**Red Letters.**" Most Bibles today will write the words that Jesus spoke in "**Red Letters**." Here in this text, as previously mentioned, Christ's words appear in bold.

"You, Lead, Lord" Notes

Chapter Three
Believe

To understand belief or to believe, is to have confidence and reliance that what is said or written is the truth.

John 6:47 **"Most assuredly, I say to you, he who believes in Me has everlasting life."** (NKJV)

John 3:16 **"For God so loved the world that He gave His only begotten Son, that whoever believes in Him should not perish but have *everlasting* life."** (NKJV, emphasis added)

If I believe in Jesus, I will have _ETERNAL_ life.

John 8:24 **"Therefore I said to you that you will die in your sins; for if you**

do not *believe* that I am He, you will *die* in your sins." (NKJV, emphasis added)

Jesus said: "If I do not _BELIEVE_ in Him I will _DIE_ in my sins."

It is vital to note who is speaking in each of these quotes. It is Jesus, laying down the truth. He reaffirms throughout Scripture that we must believe Jesus is who He claims to be and He is the only way. When you can say, "I believe Jesus is the Son of God, He is the way, the truth, and the life, and He is the only way to the Father," then all that remains to do is what He commands concerning God's promises of Heaven.

Scripture references:

Romans 1:16 "For I am not ashamed of the gospel of Christ, for it is the power of God to salvation for everyone who believes, for the Jew first and also for the Greek." (NKJV)

1 John 5:5 "Who is he who overcomes the world, but he who believes that Jesus is the Son of God?" (NKJV)

Examples of believing:

John 2:22 "Therefore, when He had risen from the dead, His disciples remembered that He had said this to them; and they believed the Scripture and the word which Jesus had said." (NKJV)

John 4:53 "So the father knew that it was at the same hour in which Jesus said to him, **'Your son lives.'** And he himself believed, and his whole household." (NKJV)

Acts 4:3–4 "And they laid hands on them, and put them in custody until the next day, for it was already evening. However, many of those who heard the word believed; and the number of the men came to be about five thousand." (NKJV)

Acts 8:13 "Then Simon himself

also believed; and when he was baptized he continued with Philip, and was amazed, seeing the miracles and signs which were done." (NKJV)

James 2:19 "You believe that there is one God. You do well. Even the demons believe—and tremble!" (NKJV)

There is more to salvation than just belief. If belief is all that is needed then the demons will be in heaven with us. We can accept and believe, or we can choose not to believe what Jesus and the Bible is so clear about.

Believe Notes

Chapter Four
Repentance

In the New Testament, repentance is realizing sin is in our life and having a desire to seek God's forgiveness. This involves a deep sorrow for past sin or wrongdoing.

Luke 13:3 "**I tell you, no; but unless you *repent* you will all likewise *perish*.**" (NKJV, emphasis added)

Jesus said, unless I __REPENT__ I will __PERISH__. What is the lesson Jesus desires for us to learn? What happens if we do not repent? Jesus is the only one who can pay the debt of sin.

A direct command from Jesus is to repent.

Repentance may be the result of God-given fear of the consequences of sin. Known sin that is not forgiven is alive and leads to an ever-widening separation between you and God. It makes no difference, whether in a worldly setting or in the spiritual setting. Sin destroys.

God's forgiveness of our repentant sin is the example we are to follow in forgiving others. Can you imagine what this world would be like and your life would be like if the anchor (or weight) of not being forgiven was completely and fully removed from your life? What would your life be like if you held nothing against loved ones, the people you work beside, and the ones you can't stand to be around? Should we not respond to those who have sinned against us the same way God responds to us when we repent?

So how important is repentance in

regard to salvation, life, and a God-like character? Jesus' words are more moving than dynamite.

Luke 13:3 **"I tell you, no; but unless you repent you will all likewise perish."** (NKJV)

He gives us no choice. We are bound by His command. There is no option; there is no other path to take. This is one essential step toward salvation.

Have you sinned? I have asked hundreds of people this question, and have yet to find one person who says they have never sinned. Once we have sinned, we have no other option—we must repent.

When sin is confessed to God and repentance is of the heart, a desire to forsake sin will be humbling. That, in turn, leads to self-surrender to God. If you want to clean your life up and get right with God, then give it all to Him.

Scripture references:

Matthew 3:1–2 "In those days John the Baptist came preaching in the wilderness of Judea, and saying, "Repent, for the kingdom of heaven is at hand!" (NKJV)

Mark 1:15 " . . . and saying, **'The time is fulfilled, and the kingdom of God is at hand. Repent, and believe in the gospel.'"** (NKJV)

Acts 3:19 "Repent therefore and be converted, that your sins may be blotted out, so that times of refreshing may come from the presence of the Lord . . ." (NKJV)

The single hardest step we are to take may be to repent. I believe the hardest person to forgive is myself. However, when we repent, Jesus lifts the load off our shoulders and places it on His.

Repentance Notes

Chapter Five
Confess

When we confess Christ, we acknowledge, concede, declare and admit we believe He is who He says He is.

Matthew 10:32–33 **"Therefore whoever *confesses* Me before men, him I will also *confess* before My Father who is in heaven. But whoever *denies* Me before men, him I will also *deny* before My Father who is in heaven."** (NKJV, emphasis added)

If I <u>CONFESS</u> Jesus, He will <u>CONFESS</u> me. If I <u>DENY</u> Jesus, He will <u>DENY</u> me.

Mark 8:37–38 **"Or what will a man give in exchange for his soul? For**

whoever is ashamed of Me and My words in this adulterous and sinful generation, of him the Son of Man also will be ashamed when He comes in the glory of His Father with the holy angels." (NKJV)

1 John 2:21–23 "I have not written to you because you do not know the truth, but because you know it, and that no lie is of the truth. Who is a liar but he who denies that Jesus is the Christ? He is antichrist who denies the Father and the Son. Whoever denies the Son does not have the Father either; he who acknowledges the Son has the Father also." (NKJV)

1 John 4:15 "Whoever confesses that Jesus is the Son of God, God abides in him, and he in God." (NKJV)

Examples of confessing Jesus:

Peter:

Matthew 16:16–17 Simon Peter answered and said, "You are the Christ, the Son of the living God." Jesus answered and said to him, **"Blessed are you, Simon Bar-Jonah, for flesh and blood has not revealed this to you, but My Father who is in heaven."** (NKJV)

John 6:68–69 But Simon Peter answered Him, "Lord, to whom shall we go? You have the words of eternal life. Also we have come to believe and know that You are the Christ, the Son of the living God." (NKJV)

Nathanael:

John 1:48–49 "Nathanael said to Him, 'How do You know me?' Jesus answered and said to him, **'Before Philip**

called you, when you were under the fig tree, I saw you.' Nathanael answered and said to Him, 'Rabbi, You are the Son of God! You are the King of Israel!'" (NKJV)

Martha:

John 11:27 "She said to Him, 'Yes, Lord, I believe that You are the Christ, the Son of God, who is to come into the world.'" (NKJV)

Thomas:

John 20:28 "And Thomas answered and said to Him, 'My Lord and my God!'" (NKJV)

One day we will all confess Jesus:

Romans 14:10–12 "But why do you judge your brother? Or why do you show contempt for your brother? For we shall all stand before the judgment seat of Christ. For it is written: 'As I live', says the LORD, 'Every knee shall bow to Me, and every tongue shall confess to God.' So then each of us shall give account of himself to God." (NKJV)

Philippians 2:10–11 " . . . that at the name of Jesus every knee should bow, of those in heaven, and of those on earth, and of those under the earth, and that every tongue should confess that Jesus Christ is Lord, to the glory of God the Father." (NKJV)

Shortly after I accepted Jesus as my Lord at the age of thirty, I met some of my friends on the street. They asked why they hadn't seen me at the bar, and in the card and pool tournaments. I simply told them I was trying to change my life for the better and was now attending church. I believe I was confessing Jesus.

People can choose to do one of two things: to confess Jesus, or *not* to confess Jesus. If we confess to Jesus and to others, then He will acknowledge us on our judgment day.

Confess Notes

Chapter Six
Baptism

To understand the Biblical meaning of baptism, we must go back to the original New Testament Greek. The definition of baptism in the Greek is very distinct—to dip, plunge under or immerse.

Matthew 3:16–17 "When He had been baptized, Jesus came up immediately from the water; and behold, the heavens were opened to Him, and He saw the Spirit of God descending like a dove and alighting upon Him. And suddenly a voice came from heaven, saying, 'This is My beloved Son, in whom I am well pleased.'" (NKJV)

How is Jesus teaching here? He

teaches by example that baptism is important and it pleases God. Jesus Himself, being God, was baptized. Remember in John 14:6 when Jesus said, **"I am the way"?** If He is truly the only way to the Father, then I desire to follow His example.

Matthew 28:18–20 "And Jesus came and spoke to them, saying, '**All authority has been given to Me in heaven and on earth. Go therefore and make disciples of all the nations, baptizing them in the name of the Father and of the Son and of the Holy Spirit, teaching them to observe all things that I have commanded you; and lo, I am with you always, even to the end of the age.**' Amen." (NKJV)

Jesus is giving final instructions to His students.

- He assures them He has all authority—not some authority, but over everything.
- He tells them to go to all nations and to make disciples (followers).
- His command is to baptize them in the name of the Father and of the Son and of the Holy Spirit. This is a "**Red Letter**" command—not a suggestion.

Mark 16:15–16 And He said to them, **"Go into all the world and preach the gospel to every creature. He who believes and is baptized will be saved; but he who does not believe will be condemned."** (NKJV)

Is baptism important to Jesus?

(Yes)　　No

There is a great deal of controversy about the way we should be baptized and whether the method really makes a difference. Our desire is to follow the Bible. In our culture today, there are three popular views as to how we should be baptized. These views differ between being sprinkled, poured upon, or immersed. However, we are not to follow culture or popular views, but we are to follow God's instruction manual—the Bible—to tell us the way.

Romans 6:3–5 "Or do you not know that as many of us as were baptized into Christ Jesus were baptized into His death? Therefore we were buried with Him through baptism into death, that just as Christ was raised from the dead by the glory of the Father, even so we also should walk in newness of life. For if we have been united together in the likeness of His death, certainly we also shall be in the likeness of His resurrection." (NKJV)

When Paul wrote to the Roman Christians, he makes it quite clear that all who were baptized were buried. Let me ask you this. If your dog died and you were going to bury it in the backyard, how would you do it? Would you lay your dog down and pour a little dirt over it, sprinkle a little dirt on it, or would you dig a hole and completely cover the dog?

Colossians 2:12 " . . . buried with Him in baptism, in which you also were raised with Him through faith in the working of God, who raised Him from the dead." (NKJV)

In the Greek language, from which the New Testament was translated, the word "baptize" means "to dip, plunge under, or immerse." If you look up baptize in the Webster's Dictionary it may say sprinkling or pouring, but look close for a '*gr.*' This is the icon for Greek. Following the '*gr.*', you will see the word 'immerse'. The words for 'sprinkle' or 'pour' in the Greek are never used in the Bible concerning baptism. In instances where the word 'baptize' appears in the Bible, you can replace it with 'immerse'.

Baptism Notes

Chapter Seven
Infant Baptism

The question I hear so often is, "I was baptized as an infant—isn't that good enough?" We have just looked at what Jesus commands.

My questions:

- When you were baptized as an infant, did you believe that Jesus is the Son of God?
- Did you repent?
- Did you confess Jesus as your Lord?
- How were you taught about Jesus?
- When you were baptized were you sprinkled, poured or immersed?

The reason most people are baptized as infants is for one of two reasons.

1. The teaching that an infant inherits Adam's sin, or even the sins of their father.
2. The parents or church desire it.

Let us see what scripture says.

Ezekiel 18:20 "The soul who sins shall die. The son shall not bear the guilt of the father, nor the father bear the guilt of the son. The righteousness of the righteous shall be upon himself, and the wickedness of the wicked shall be upon himself." (NKJV)

This is a clear statement. We are charged or credited with the choices we make. We are not charged with Adam's sin, but with our own sin. God does not hold people responsible for the action of others. Each one of us will answer for the choices we make each day.

Deuteronomy 24:16 "Fathers shall not be put to death for their children, nor shall children be put to death for their fathers; a person shall be put to death for his *own* sin." (NKJV, emphasis added)

Each is to die for his ___OWN___ sin.

The second reason why babies are baptized is because the parents or church desire it. Who is making the decision or choice? Is it the one who is being baptized, or someone else? God desires each of us to make our own choice. Do I want my salvation to rely solely on the choice my parents made for me?

We need to make our own choice when we understand right from wrong, good from evil, having an understanding of sin, God's love, God's grace, and of Heaven and Hell.

Mark 16:15–16 And He said to them, **"Go into all the world and preach the gospel to every creature. He who believes and is baptized will be saved; but he who does not believe will be condemned."** (NKJV)

The gospel must be preached and understood before baptism. The one being baptized must believe. Ask yourself, "How can infants show their faith? How can infants be taught about Christ?"

Luke 13:3 **"I tell you, no; but unless you repent you will all likewise perish."** (NKJV)

If repentance must take place in order to be saved, how can infants repent if they cannot understand the concept of sin?

Matthew 10:32–33 **"Therefore whoever *confesses* Me before men, him I will also *confess* before My Father who**

is in heaven. But whoever denies Me before men, him I will also deny before My Father who is in heaven." (NKJV, emphasis added)

The person being baptized must make a confession of their faith in Christ. Confession is not possible for infants.

The following questions need to be asked if considering infant baptism:

- What does God's word teach? (Ezekiel 18:20; Deuteronomy 24:16 & John 9:1–3)
- Where is an example in the Bible of infant baptism?
- How can you teach a baby to analyze spiritual concepts?
- How can a baby believe, repent, confess, and express a desire for baptism?
- Where is choice?
- Do babies who die at birth or before birth spend eternity in Hell?

I want to make my own choice for my salvation based upon fact. Do you? When someone else makes my decisions or choices for me, I trust them for my consequence. What if they are wrong?

I have heard some say, "There must have been infants in the families of the household baptisms mentioned in the book of Acts." Before we assume there were infants baptized, let's take a closer look. There are four cases of *household* baptism mentioned in the New Testament, and there is proof that in three of these that no infants were baptized.

- In the case of Cornelius' household, all who were *baptized* believe and spoke in tongues. (Acts 10:46–11:17)
- In the case of the Philippian jailer, all those who were *baptized,* rejoiced and believed. (Acts 16:34)
- In the case of Stephanas, they devoted

themselves to ministry after they were *baptized.* (I Corinthians 1:16 & 16:15)
- In the case of Lydia, to assume there were infants when there is no evidence, is to go against all Jesus taught and the examples of the other household baptisms. (Acts 16:14–15)

In the *"household"* baptisms that are elaborated on in the New Testament, it is clearly shown that these conditions were present. The *baptized* were *hearers, believers, and penitent.* They rejoiced and they served.

Should infants be baptized? The answer is "yes" if we can show:
- One example in the New Testament where infants were *baptized,* and—
- That they met and understood the prerequisites of belief, confession, and repentance required of those baptized in the New Testament.

But the Biblical facts are:
- That there is not one case of *"infant baptism"* in the New Testament.
- The logical conclusion from the Biblical evidence is that babies are:
- Born into this world without the personal guilt of their ancestors.
- Not lost and in need of salvation.
- Safe until they reach an accountable age where they become guilty of their sins, and in need of salvation.
- What if you were "*baptized*" as an infant?
- Most likely you were not actually *baptized* by immersion, but simply 'sprinkled'.
- Even if immersed, it was not *"Bible baptism"* which requires belief, repentance, and confession.

Thus, you are still in need of obeying the Word of the Lord! Don't place your faith in the traditions of men or in the doctrines of some church. Place your faith in God's Word, and obey it accordingly!

Infant Baptism Notes

Chapter Eight
Sinner's Prayer

Here's an example of a sinner's prayer. (Many have been written.)

"Lord Jesus, I am a sinner. But I believe that You died upon the cross for me. That You shed Your precious blood for the forgiveness of my sin. And I believe that on the third day, You rose from the dead, and went to Heaven to prepare a place for me. I accept You now as my Savior, my Lord, my God, my friend. Come into my heart, Lord Jesus, and set me free from my sin. And, because You are my Savior, Jesus, "I shall not die, but have everlasting life." Thank You, Jesus, for saving me!"

Let's take a Biblical look at the

"Sinner's Prayer". The "Sinner's Prayer" is not found anywhere among the conversions in the New Testament. There is not one instance of any sinner (non-Christian) instructed to pray for their salvation. (New Testament conversions are listed in Chapter Nine of this document.)

Matthew 7:21 **"Not everyone who says to Me, 'Lord, Lord,' shall enter the kingdom of heaven, but he who does the will of My Father in heaven."** (NKJV)

Luke 6:46 **"But why do you call Me 'Lord, Lord,' and not do the things which I say?"** (NKJV)

The Scripture that is used most often to solidify the claims that one can have salvation by repeating a prayer is found in Romans 10:9–10.

Romans 10:9–10 " . . . that if you confess with your mouth the Lord Jesus and believe in your heart that God has raised Him from the dead, you will be saved. For with the heart one believes unto righteousness, and with the mouth confession is made unto salvation." (NKJV)

First we must determine to whom *Romans* is written.

Romans 1:7 "To all who are in Rome, beloved of God, called to be saints: Grace to you and peace from God our Father and the Lord Jesus Christ." (NKJV)

Romans 6:3 "Or do you not know that as many of us as were baptized into Christ Jesus were baptized into His death?" (NKJV)

Romans was written to the Christians in Rome. If we only stand on this Scripture for our salvation, we leave out repentance and baptism. However, if we have been obedient in all Jesus' commands for salvation (believe, confess, repent, and baptized) and then do as this verse states, it all makes perfect sense. As a Christian, if I believe and confess, I will be saved.

We know what Jesus tells us to do for salvation. The sinner's prayer is man-made and goes against what Scripture teaches. Now the question is—will we follow what Jesus tells us, or what man tells us?

Sinner's Prayer Notes

Chapter Nine
From Non-Christian To Christian In The Bible

Acts 2:36–38 "Therefore let all the house of Israel know assuredly that God has made this Jesus, whom you crucified, both Lord and Christ." Now when they heard this, they were cut to the heart, and said to Peter and the rest of the apostles, "Men and brethren, what shall we do?" Then Peter said to them, "Repent, and let every one of you be baptized in the name of Jesus Christ for the remission of sins; and you shall receive the gift of the Holy Spirit." (NKJV)

Acts 8:12 "But when they believed Philip as he preached the things concerning the kingdom of God and the name of Jesus Christ, both men and women were baptized." (NKJV)

Acts 8:34–38 "So the eunuch answered Philip and said, 'I ask you, of whom does the prophet say this, of himself or of some other man?' Then Philip opened his mouth, and beginning at this Scripture, preached Jesus to him. Now as they went down the road, they came to some water. And the eunuch said, 'See, here is water. What hinders me from being baptized?' Then Philip said, 'If you believe with all your heart, you may.' And he answered and said, 'I believe that Jesus Christ is the Son of God.' So he commanded the chariot to stand still. And both Philip and the eunuch went down into the water, and he baptized him." (NKJV)

Acts 9:18 "Immediately there fell from his eyes something like scales, and he received his sight at once; and he arose and was baptized." (NKJV)

Acts 10:43–48 "To Him all the prophets witness that, through His name, whoever believes in Him will receive remission of sins. While Peter was still speaking these words, the Holy Spirit fell upon all those who heard the word. And those of the circumcision who believed were astonished, as many as came with Peter, because the gift of the Holy Spirit had been poured out on the Gentiles also. For they heard them speak with tongues and magnify God. Then Peter answered, 'Can anyone forbid water, that these should not be baptized who have received the Holy Spirit just as we have?' And he commanded them to be baptized in the name of the Lord. Then they asked him to stay a few days." (NKJV)

Acts 16:14-15 "Now a certain

woman named Lydia heard us. She was a seller of purple from the city of Thyatira, who worshiped God. The Lord opened her heart to heed the things spoken by Paul. And when she and her household were baptized, she begged us, saying, 'If you have judged me to be faithful to the Lord, come to my house and stay.' So she persuaded us." (NKJV)

Acts 16:27–34 "And the keeper of the prison, awaking from sleep and seeing the prison doors open, supposing the prisoners had fled, drew his sword and was about to kill himself. But Paul called with a loud voice, saying, 'Do yourself no harm, for we are all here.' Then he called for a light, ran in, and fell down trembling before Paul and Silas. And he brought them out and said, 'Sirs, what must I do to be saved?' So they said, 'Believe on the Lord Jesus Christ, and you will be saved, you and your household.' Then they spoke the word of the Lord to him and to all who were in his house. And he took them the same hour of the night and washed their stripes. And immediately he and all his family were baptized. Now when he had brought them into his house, he set food before them; and he rejoiced, having believed in God with all his household." (NKJV)

Acts 18:8 "Then Crispus, the ruler of the synagogue, believed on the Lord with all his household. And many of the Corinthians, hearing, believed and were baptized." (NKJV)

Acts 19:2–5 " . . . he said to them, 'Did you receive the Holy Spirit when you believed?' So they said to him, 'We have not so much as heard whether there is a Holy Spirit.' And he said to them, 'Into what then were you baptized?' So they said, 'Into John's baptism.' Then Paul said, 'John indeed baptized with a baptism of repentance, saying to the people that they should believe on Him who would come after him, that is, on Christ Jesus.' When they heard this, they were baptized in the name of the Lord Jesus." (NKJV)

Acts 22:1–16 " 'Brethren and fathers, hear my defense before you now.' And when they heard that he spoke to them in the Hebrew language, they kept all the more silent. Then he said: 'I am indeed a Jew, born in Tarsus of Cilicia, but brought up in this city at the feet of Gamaliel, taught according to the strictness of our fathers' law, and was zealous toward God as you all are today. I persecuted this Way to the death, binding and delivering into prisons both men and women, as also the high priest bears me witness, and all the council of the elders, from whom I also received letters to the brethren, and went to Damascus to bring in chains even those who were there to Jerusalem to be punished. "Now it happened, as I journeyed and came near Damascus at about noon, suddenly a great light from heaven shone around me. And I fell to the ground and heard a voice saying to me, 'Saul, Saul, why are you persecuting Me?' So I answered, 'Who are You, Lord?' And He said to me, 'I am Jesus of Nazareth, whom you are persecuting.' "And those who were with me indeed saw the light and were afraid, but they did not hear the voice of Him who spoke to me. So I said, 'What shall I do, Lord?' And the Lord said to me, 'Arise and go into Damascus, and there you will be told all things which are appointed for you to do.' And since I could not see for the glory of that light, being led by the hand of those who were with me, I came into Damascus. "Then a certain Ananias, a devout man according to the law, having a good testimony with all the Jews who dwelt there, came to me; and he stood and said to me, 'Brother Saul, receive your sight.' And at that same hour I looked up at him. Then he said, 'The God of our fathers has chosen you that you should know His will, and see the Just One, and hear the voice of His mouth. For you will be His witness to all men of what you have seen and heard. And now why are you waiting? Arise and be baptized, and wash away your sins, calling on the name of the Lord.'" (NKJV)

From Non-Christian to Christian in the Bible Notes

SALVATION

Conclusion

I had a very good friend tell me once, concerning salvation, "It's a simple plan for complicated people." I agree. What more do you want God to do for you so you can have Heaven and not Hell? What more could Jesus do to prove His love for you?

We have a tendency to want to follow man's teaching instead of following God's simple plan. Would you agree that with each generation we seem to be getting further from the simplicity of Biblical truth?

Why not stand on what Jesus commands and not add to or take away from

His word? This is expressed by Paul in Galatians 1:8–10 and 2 Corinthians 11:3–4 as a warning about following any teaching other than that of Jesus Christ.

Galatians 1:8–10 "But even if we, or an angel from heaven, preach any other gospel to you than what we have preached to you, let him be accursed. As we have said before, so now I say again, if anyone preaches any other gospel to you than what you have received, let him be accursed. For do I now persuade men, or God? Or do I seek to please men? For if I still pleased men, I would not be a bondservant of Christ." (NKJV)

2 Corinthians 11:3–4 "But I fear, lest somehow, as the serpent deceived Eve by his craftiness, so your minds may be corrupted from the simplicity that is in Christ. For if he who comes preaches another Jesus whom we have not preached, or if

you receive a different spirit which you have not received, or a different gospel which you have not accepted—you may well put up with it!" (NKJV)

Have we been deceived by the serpent's cunning ways? Do we follow a different Gospel when we teach sprinkling, pouring, infant baptism, or saying a prayer for salvation? If not, where is this taught, or where is an example of these teachings in God's Holy Bible?

The hardest question we may have to answer is asked by Jesus in Luke 6:46. **"But why do you call Me 'Lord, Lord,' and not do the things which I say?"** (NKJV)

All the belief, confessing, repenting, and baptizing is of no avail if we do not live as Christians, if we do not seek and nourish a relationship with Jesus. These commands listed here are the first steps, of your Christian walk. Our actions must come from a pure heart, understanding all that Jesus did for us and all He desires for us. Jesus' commands are an open invitation to a love relationship with Him and His Father.

The last instruction Jesus gives his students in Matthew is how I would like to end this study:

Matthew 28:18–20 "And Jesus came and spoke to them, saying, '**All authority has been given to Me in heaven and on earth. Go therefore and make disciples of all the nations, baptizing them in the name of the Father and of the Son and of the Holy Spirit, teaching them to observe all things that I have commanded you; and lo, I am with you always, even to the end of the age.**' Amen." (NKJV)

Jesus assures us that He has all

authority, not some authority, but *all*. All is all, complete authority in heaven and on earth. Next, He tells us to *go*. We are to *tell others* of His love and authority. Isn't it interesting that the first word in the last verse in the gospel of Matthew is a command *to teach?* Teaching is never to stop. We are to *teach* and be *taught.* The salvation message does not stop at belief, confession, repenting or baptism. Jesus loved you enough to die for you. Our life is one of striving to become more like our Lord.

As we grow in Christ we will understand the love God has for us. May we have the same desire as Paul in Philippians 3:7–11, "But what things were gain to me, these I have counted loss for Christ. Yet indeed I also count all things loss for the excellence of the knowledge of Christ Jesus my Lord, for whom I have suffered the loss of all things, and count them as rubbish, that I may gain Christ and be found in Him, not having my own righteousness, which is from the law, but that which is through faith in Christ, the righteousness which is from God by faith; that I may know Him and the power of His resurrection, and the fellowship of His sufferings, being conformed to His death, if, by any means, I may attain to the resurrection from the dead." (NKJV)

I pray to God that what I have written here is His truth and that His blessings will enrich your life as you desire to be obedient to the simple gospel truth.

Marshall Smith

May I be conformed to His death daily in my flesh, so that my spirit can soar.

Order more copies of this book at

TATE PUBLISHING, LLC

127 East Trade Center Terrace
Mustang, OK 73064

(888) 361 - 9473

Tate Publishing, LLC

www.tatepublishing.com